Llywodraeth Cynulliad Cymru
Welsh Assembly Government

Wales. World Nation.

Welsh Assembly Government
Cathays Park
Cardiff
CF10 3NQ

www.walesworldnation.com

Llywodraeth Cynulliad Cymru
Parc Cathays
Caerdydd
CF10 3NQ

ISBN: 0 7504 2623 3

February 2004
Chwefror 2004

FOREWORD

Mae'n bleser gennyf i gyflwyno Gymru: Cymru newydd, ein Cymru ni.

I have great pleasure in introducing you to Wales: a new Wales, our Wales. This land possesses a rich and unique heritage, a special language and culture, a stunning range of landscapes and a practical, resourceful people of unmatched character.

Some describe Wales as one of Europe's best-kept secrets. That is changing; Wales is taking its rightful place on the world stage. We are coming out of the shadows with a great story to tell the world what Wales is about: a special place that is full of history, but also a new country with new optimism and a system of domestic self-government that symbolises our new self-confidence. We are proud of our history and at the same time we look forward to the challenges ahead. We are confident that our talents will carry us to a more prosperous and sustainable future.

Wales is a dynamic and innovative nation. Our language, culture, history and institutions have helped to make Wales a distinctive country. We are home to iconic buildings such as the world-famous Millennium Stadium and the Wales Millennium Centre, a new home for, amongst others, the Welsh National Opera. Our track record of attracting companies to set up in Wales is second to none, and is clear proof of the qualities that our country and our people have to offer.

The challenge facing us now is to strengthen our international, commercial and cultural links and to increase our presence in a global market. I am confident that the spirit of the Welsh people, which shines through in this book, will ensure that we succeed and take our rightful place as "Wales. World Nation."

Rhodri Morgan AM
First Minister
Welsh Assembly Government
February 2004

CONTENTS

Chapter one
A NEW AGE DAWNS

"Every day when I wake up I thank the Lord I'm Welsh"

From "International Velvet" Mark Roberts/Catatonia 1998

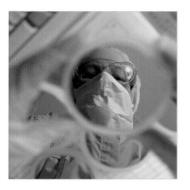

For some, the past is another country, but not for Wales. We are one of the newest democracies in Europe,

and we are the only country in the world to enter the third millennium with the same national flag as when

we entered the second millennium.

The establishment of the National Assembly for Wales is helping us to build our confidence to face the future.

That future is based on the rich platform of our distinctive Celtic language, literature and musical culture.

Wales is emerging from its heavily industrialised past as a technologically advanced nation. New industries

based in Wales such as optronics, and aerospace software are thriving, as are even newer ones:

telecommunications and the development of semiconductor wafers more advanced than the silicon chip.

Their success is encouraged by the Welsh Development Agency, which focuses on nurturing enterprises in

Wales, while continuing to encourage inward investment.

(previous) Sculpture Fountain, Cardiff Bay, South Wales
(left) Visual Inspection of completed wing, Airbus UK, Broughton, North Wales
(above, top) IQE Ltd, St Mellons, South Wales, suppliers of specialised compound semiconductor wafers
(above, lower) Working on an aeroplane, British Airways Maintenance Cardiff, Cardiff International Airport, South Wales

The scars that the industrial revolution and extractive industries left on the Welsh landscape have almost

healed, with huge land reclamation and recovery projects already completed and more planned.

We have the only coastal national park in the United Kingdom. Over 22km of old coastline in

Carmarthenshire, West Wales has been transformed into a remarkable new Millennium Coastal Park. Wales

is already blessed with awe-inspiring landscapes and a beautiful coastline rich in marine wildlife, sandy

coves, and beaches safe for sailing and surfing; new developments such as this should help ensure that

everyone in Wales can continue to enjoy the beauty and tranquillity that have so inspired poets and painters

from Wales and all over the world.

Porthdinllaen on Llyn Peninsula, North Wales

We are as proud of our past as we are optimistic about our future.

Achieving enduring success as a nation means life-long learning embedded in the Welsh way of life.

In a knowledge-driven world, everyone will need the skills and knowledge to fulfil their potential throughout

their lives. We in Wales have always put the highest value on education.

Originally education in Wales meant the means to escape life underground in the mine or on the hill farm,

now it is about acquiring the qualifications to compete in a global economy. Our schools, colleges and

universities provide the foundation that is our economic strength.

(left) **Modern Apprentice at Bearing Technologies, Mid Wales**   *(above, top)* **Barry College, South Wales**
(above, lower) **Ysgol y Creuddyn, Llandudno, North Wales**

Golden Grove, Carmarthen

If I might where I pleased compose my nest,

The Golden Grove should be my constant rest.

This curious fabric might make us believe

That angels there, or men like angels, live.

I must commend the outside; but within

Not to admire, it were almost a sin.

Of fertile ground the large circumference

With admiration may confound the sense;

Which ground, if things were rightly understood, From paradise came tumbling in the flood,

And there the water left it, therefore we

Find here of pleasures such variety.

Wise Nature here did strive, and witty Art,

To please the curious eye and longing heart.

Taken from a poem by Rowland Watkyns (circa 1600)

A performance in Cardiff, South Wales

Chapter two
WALES. A NEW DEMOCRACY

"Wales says Yes!"

Headline from "Western Mail", 19 September 1997

15

The people of Wales voted for their own Assembly in a referendum on 18 September 1997. Direct elections for it were held on 6th May 1999, and the first actions of the new National Assembly for Wales took place in the plenary session of 12th May 1999. After 600 years, political decisions affecting Wales are once again being decided by an organisation elected exclusively by the people of Wales.

The Assembly works to develop and implement policies that relate specifically to Wales. It is committed to being

open and has adopted many new ways of working, including proportional representation in Assembly

elections. There are 60 Assembly Members (AM), with 40 representing their constituencies and 20 their

regions. The Assembly is developing its policies and actions though informed partnerships with the public,

private and voluntary sectors in Wales, as well as seeking to build strong and enduring relationships with key

organisations in Europe and beyond.

(above) The new building for the National Assembly for Wales, Cardiff, South Wales

The Welsh Assembly Government is keen to exert influence on a whole range of issues that can affect people

and businesses in Wales.

For example, the Wales Trade International team hosts and sends delegations around the world aiming

to increase trade. The National Assembly for Wales is also a member of the Commonwealth

Parliamentary Association.

The Welsh Assembly Government has also set-up a permanent office in Brussels, with diplomatic status. Staff

work, with partners, to facilitate the Assembly's growing involvement with European Union policy making.

Wales is rapidly becoming an active partner in the European family and the Brussels link provides us with a

channel for developing new relationships.

Case Study European Summit

In June 1998, the 15 heads of the countries in the European Union, together with the world's media, arrived in Cardiff for the European Summit that marked the end of the UK's presidency of the European Union. While the leaders gathered for their final discussions in City Hall, Nelson Mandela received an enthusiastic welcome from the thousands of local people who had gathered to welcome him to Cardiff Castle.

Gobal competition and new technologies are reshaping our economy, altering the nature of work and

having a powerful effect on all of our lives. With unprecedented challenges come unique opportunities.

Just as our ancestors emerged from the crucible of industrialisation stronger and wiser, we are confident that

Wales will grow from strength to strength, with an improved lifestyle, environment and economy.

The Welsh Assembly Government is already working to help turn our vision into reality; to deliver a distinctly

Welsh approach to the issues we all face. By working in partnership with others, focussing on those areas

which can make a real difference and by creating a society in which achievement is applauded, everyone in

Wales is facing the future with anticipation.

(left) Children at Ysgol Gymraeg Casnewydd, South Wales, one of the many schools in Wales where
pupils are taught all their subjects in Welsh

Chapter three
LAND OF INNOVATION

" The Red Dragon will show the way "

Deio ab leuan Du, c.1450

23

For generations, we have prided ourselves on our innovation and ability to generate new ideas. From the

first railway to the first optical fibre, Wales has shown the way. Even the world's first canned beer came from

Wales. Now, the same tradition of design skills includes Welsh spring water bottled in a distinctive award-

winning blue bottle which can be found in almost every top quality hotel in the world; a local, top quality

product which capitalises on the growth in popularity of organic foods; and world famous clothing designs.

(previous page) Angharad Jones, born in North Wales, specialises in producing organic/feminine forms from large pieces of forged, shaped and fabricated steel, adding colour and industrial sections
(left) The distinctive blue bottle of Ty Nant Spring water, sourced and bottled in Mid Wales
(above, top) A selection of cheeses from Wales
(above, lower) Organic yoghurts being produced at Rachel's Dairy, Aberystwyth, Mid Wales

Case Study Sky Dome, Welsh School of Architecture

The largest artificial sky in Britain, the £200,000 Sky Dome can simulate sky conditions at any time of day in any part of the world, from overcast skies at dawn to brilliant afternoon sunshine. The eight metre rig, with 640 lamps is used by architects for a number of environmental applications such as maximising the use of natural light in a building, reducing the use of electric lights and controlling solar radiation.

In Wales, we have a tradition of seeking original solutions to problems. Sometimes this expresses itself in new inventions, and sometimes in being innovative in our response to changing times. One hundred and fifty years ago, we built the largest ironworks anywhere in the world. The biggest slate mine in the world was in Wales. Today we have transformed a redundant coal mine into a major tourist attraction; and the importance of our industrial heritage has been recognised universally by the award of "World Heritage Site" status to the old iron and coal-producing district of Blaenavon. This was also the location of an example of 19th century Welsh innovation, namely the collaboration between Sidney Gilchrist Thomas and his cousin that followed Thomas's experiments with Bessemer converter linings for steel production. Patented in 1877, the Thomas Process was used for nearly a century. The opening of the Second Severn Crossing, a spectacular engineering achievement that has noticeably improved communications between Wales and England is evidence of our innovation today. The Welsh coal industry is now one coal mine, proudly run by the coal-miners. Tower Colliery has inspired the people of Wales with its can-do spirit. This positive attitude prevails at every level in Welsh society and promises a long and progressive period of achievement.

(left) Pit Head, Big Pit, Blaenavon, South Wales   *(above, top)* Visitors to Big Pit, Blaenavon, South Wales
(above, lower) Biotransformation and biodegradation at the University of Wales, Aberystwyth

Perhaps more than anywhere in Europe, the Welsh economy has shifted dramatically away from heavy

industry towards 21st-century technology, including the ever-expanding communications and service

industries. As a consequence, Wales has become a focal point for media and multi-media activity. In recent

years two Welsh films have been nominated for Best Foreign Language Oscars®: these were "Hedd Wyn" in

1994 and "Solomon and Gaenor" in 2000. Several major animated films have also been

commissioned in Wales including the Oscar®-nominated "The Canterbury Tales".

The innovative and flexible character of the Welsh people has also made Wales one of the leading countries

for foreign direct investment. In 2002 more than 60,000 Welsh workers were employed by over 300

international manufacturing companies.

Case Study Moving pictures from Wales

Animated film and TV productions such as "The Canterbury Tales" (main picture) and "The Miracle Maker" (inset left) have received worldwide acclaim. Masterminded by Christopher Grace of S4C, they have been created by the skills of the greatest animators in Wales and Russia, using cutting-edge 2D, 3D and computer techniques.

(above, top) **Animation work at Cartwn Cymru** *(above, lower)* **Scene from Oscar-nominated film, Hedd Wyn**

The will to succeed can be seen in many aspects of Welsh life. Take the legendary Thrust supersonic car that

broke the world land speed record. Few people know that it was perfected using research carried out at the

Department of Engineering at the University of Wales in Swansea.

Terry Matthews, son of a Welsh coal miner, now Wales' first billionaire, is one of the world's leading entrepreneurs

in high technology specialising in telecommunications. Dr. Chris Evans, the son of a Port Talbot steelworker, has

become the driving force behind the British biotech industry.

Wales' innovative instincts are being put to good use in many diverse and exciting ways.

(left) The Thrust Supersonic car
(above) The "Thrustcar" team at University of Wales, Swansea, from left: Professor Ken Morgan, Dr. Oubay Hassan, Professor Nigel P. Weatherill   33

Exploring new paths in the arts, science and commerce has been our life-blood for centuries.

Whilst proud of our past achievements and history, our eyes are fixed firmly on the future.

Not content to be on the outside, the Welsh people are determined to be at the centre of decision-making in

Europe and beyond.

The Technium programme illustrates the Welsh approach to innovation and originality. At 8 sites across

Wales, expertise and innovation are incorporated with state-of-the-art facilities under a single roof.

The first Technium, Swansea, South Wales

Chapter four
AN ENRICHING LIFESTYLE

"Lovely the woods, waters, meadows, combs, vales,

All the fair things that built this world of Wales."

Gerard Manley Hopkins

The diverse natural landscape of Wales offers plenty of opportunities for healthy living.

Whilst rugby football is the sport most associated with Wales, golf is increasing in popularity. The recent investment of over £100 million in the Celtic Manor Resort at Newport, South Wales, with its championship-standard golf courses is reinforcing this. The resort will host the Ryder Cup in 2010. Other sports and pastimes are also flourishing with assistance from the Sports Council for Wales, which is responsible for delivering the Welsh Assembly Government's programme for sport in Wales.

Increasing numbers of young Welsh performers are reaching excellence across a wide range of sports, including judo and sailing, and the number of individuals achieving British representation has reached an all-time high.

(previous page) Snowdonia, North Wales   *(left)* Celtic Manor Resort, South Wales
(above, top) Playing golf at Nefyn, North Wales   *(above, lower)* White Water Rafting, River Treweryn, Mid Wales

Wales can boast three spectacular National Parks, the Brecon Beacons, Snowdonia and the

Pembrokeshire Coast. There are also over 1000 Sites of Special Scientific Interest and six environmentally

sensitive areas where rare species such as the Red Kite (pictured overleaf) can thrive.

Sailing with Pen-y-Fan, Brecon Beacons, Mid Wales forming an impressive backdrop

The preservation of our native flora and fauna is a priority in Wales. The Pembrokeshire Coastal National Park,

for example, contains a reserve dedicated to the study and conservation of marine wild life. Whilst the

spectacular Snowdonia National Park is one of the largest of its kind in Europe.

Our natural attractions are also important in helping to develop our tourism business.

Case Study Skomer Island, West Wales

Lying off the south coast of Pembrokeshire, Skomer Island is an important breeding ground for a wide variety of seabirds. The 292-hectare island is protected as a national Nature Reserve, a Site of Special Scientific Interest and a Special Protection Area under European Law. Visitors are drawn to the area by the dolphins, porpoises and grey seals, as well as the 6,000 pairs of puffins which nest on the island, and its population of 165,000 pairs of Manx Shearwaters

43

(above, top) The Red Kite, a symbol of Mid Wales *(above, middle)* Angling on Tal-y-Llyn, Mid Wales
(above, lower) Bottlenose Dolphin off the coast of Pembrokeshire, West Wales

The beaches of Wales are host to all kinds of activities. Surf boarding and diving can be enjoyed side by side

with sea fishing. The flat sands at Pendine, West Wales have even been the venue of attempts on the World

Land Speed Record. We boast one of the most magnificent coastlines in Europe, and remain committed to

achieving the highest possible bathing water quality in Europe; we are already well on the way to achieving

our target of 50 Blue Flag beaches. The results, like the sea, are clear: thriving wildlife, more leisure

opportunities and increased visitors to our coasts.

Hang-gliding, Rhossili Beach, Gower, West Wales

Our snow-capped mountains, broadleaf woodlands, fast flowing rivers and dune-backed beaches

encourage a wide range of recreational pursuits.

The hundreds of natural and man-made lakes represent ideal venues for wind surfing and canoeing.

Heather-clad hills offer the opportunity to ride and roam on horseback for hours without hindrance.

While steep upland tracks present an irresistible challenge to mountain cyclists of all ages.

It is no wonder that more than one million adults in Wales enjoy sport on a regular basis.

(left) Pony Trekking, Cader Idris, North Wales   *(above, top)* Llynnau Mymbyr, Snowdonia, North Wales
(above, middle) Cyclists, Coed y Brenin, Mid Wales   *(above, lower)* Windsurfing, Dale, West Wales

Festivals are an important part of life in

Wales. The annual Hay Festival in Mid

Wales, which celebrates literature and

language, attracts writers and

audiences from around the world.

The International Eisteddfod at

Llangollen, North Wales, is also

gaining a worldwide reputation.

The Brecon Jazz festival is a

vibrant occasion, showcasing

leading international jazz

performers in the venues

throughout the town.

Scott Hamilton (saxophone) performing at the Brecon Jazz festival

While we work and play hard, we also know how to relax.

The regeneration of city centres has resulted in a rapid growth of new restaurants, cafes and bars.

They stand alongside traditional pubs and clubs to provide an outstanding choice of entertainment.

Chefs take full advantage of locally harvested produce and fresh ingredients, notably seafood, to create a

standard of cuisine that stands comparison with much of the rest of Europe.

Music also plays a significant role in Welsh life. Wales has many places where live music is performed from

classical concertos and male voice choirs to hard rock. There are also opportunities to experience some of the

world's finest performers in unique locations such as castles and stately homes.

(left) Blue Anchor Inn, Vale of Glamorgan, South Wales *(above, top)* The interior of a Brains pub, South Wales
(above, lower) Swansea Marina, West Wales

The Welsh National Opera in concert, Caernarfon Castle, North Wales

Chapter five
A POSITIVE ECONOMY

"Investing in Wales has been a decision that has

strengthened our business. From our initial introduction to

the area through the establishment of the business and

subsequent plans for expansion, we have had the support

and encouragement of all involved. The people of Wales

have made the difference"

Rocialle Medical Ltd

55

In the 18th and 19th century Wales changed from an agricultural to industrial economy, based largely on

heavy and extractive industries, coal, iron and steel.

In the last part of the twentieth century it was transformed once more, this time to aerospace, electronics and

engineering; more recently to services and software.

(left) Working on an aeroplane engine at General Electric, near Caerphilly, South Wales
(above) Single aisle wing assembly, Airbus UK, Broughton, North Wales

The commitment of our skilled workforce to manufacturing is a vital ingredient of Wales. Manufacturing

productivity rates in Wales are amongst the highest in the UK, while the costs of setting up manufacturing

capacity here are among the lowest. We also have one of the most developed infrastructures in Europe. Billions

of pounds have been spent to meet the transport and communication needs of businesses, including first class

freight services by sea, air and land. There is also a ready supply of land and property, compared with similar

regions of Europe, to ensure that prospering businesses have room to grow.

Polishing, Thales Optics, St Asaph, North Wales

"Restoration", starring Meg Ryan, seen here being filmed at Caerphilly Castle, South Wales, is one of

hundreds of feature films that have been wholly or partly filmed in Wales. The dramatic landscapes have

proven attractive to many filmmakers from David Lean with "Lawrence of Arabia" to more recently

The changes in our economy have resulted in Wales developing as the most advanced automotive supply

region in the UK. There are over 300 companies throughout Wales, employing nearly 30,000 people and

generating sales of over £2 billion a year. Ford is one of the key companies, with an engine plant at

Bridgend, South Wales and a transmission plant at Swansea, West Wales. The multi-skilled, team-based

workforce is seen as the company's industrial relations role model.

(left) The Ford factory at Bridgend produces V8 engines for Jaguar
(above, top) Trico produces wiper and wash systems at its factory in South Wales
(above, middle) INA Bearing Co Ltd produces wheel bearings at its factory at Llanelli, West Wales
(above, lower) Toyota, Deeside, North Wales

Welsh people are highly skilled and work hard. Our heritage of innovation and creativity means that

many leading companies thrive in Wales. We have world leading strengths in electronics and information

technology, with four of the world's six largest electronics manufacturers established here.

Remaining at the forefront of technology demands considerable investment in education and training;

research and development is also important, which is why 20 Centres of Excellence, covering a range of

disciplines, have been established across Wales. We were also one of the first regions in Europe to have

received European Commission funding to develop a Regional Technology Plan with the long-term objective

to help ensure that we have a culture which values and encourages innovation.

(left) North Wales-based Pinacl Communications Systems is a world-leader in the provision of products and services to upgrade or expand network infrastructures
(above) Euro DPC, Llanberis, North Wales

Around 80% of the area of Wales remains devoted to agriculture, with some 30,000 main agricultural

holdings, the majority of which are dependent on livestock production.

Our agricultural heritage was crucial in the development of our economy and landscape.

Today much attention is being devoted to improving the efficiency and profitability of the industry.

The Agri-Food Partnership has been established under the guidance of the Welsh Assembly Government to

help achieve this objective. This is adopting an approach aimed at linking the character and individuality of

Welsh food and drink producers to new market opportunities in the UK and overseas.

Our dynamic food-processing sector ranges from small producers to major multi-nationals, with seven of the

UK's top ten food processors with operations here, including Unilever and Kellogg's.

(left) Cattle judging at the Royal Welsh Show, Builth Wells, Mid Wales
(above, top) Giving consumers the opportunity to sample first-class Welsh food
(above, lower) Llanidloes market, Mid Wales

Tourism is growing in importance to the Welsh economy and has become one of our major industries. It's estimated tourism employs 100,000 people and earns £2 billion each year. With our unique culture and rich heritage we are well placed to benefit from the increase in leisure time, and growth in short-break holidays. To meet this growing demand, there has been considerable public and private investment. Oakwood Park in West Wales, for example, has one of the world's finest wooden roller coasters (and the longest in Europe), attracting enthusiasts from all over the world to sample its thrills. 5-star hotels include the Celtic Manor Resort in

Newport, the Hilton Hotel and the St. David's Hotel & Spa in Cardiff and Morgans Hotel in Swansea.

Of course, what makes any holiday special is the welcome a country gives its guests. Building on our tradition

of friendliness, the Wales Tourist Board's Welcome Host scheme is encouraging the highest standards of

customer care across the entire industry. This should help to ensure that we continue to offer the warmest of

welcomes to everyone from tourist to business person alike.

Megafobia, the wooden roller coaster at Oakwood Park, West Wales

Chapter six
TREASURING OUR PAST

"The land of my fathers is dear to me,

Land of poets and singers, men of renown"

English translation of Hen Wlad fy Nhadau

(Welsh National Anthem) Evan James 1856

Wales has a dramatic and colourful history. In the Iron Age, the land was populated by the Celts.

A warrior-like but artistic tribe, they established the first identifiable Welsh culture. In their society artistic gifts

were valued as highly as fighting skills in battle. Celtic influences remained strong, surviving the arrival of the

Romans, and even when the last prince of an independent Wales, Llewelyn ap Gruffudd, was killed in battle,

the Celtic culture continued to thrive. The Celts' love of legend, poetry and song has survived in the people of

Wales today and become an indelible part of our character.

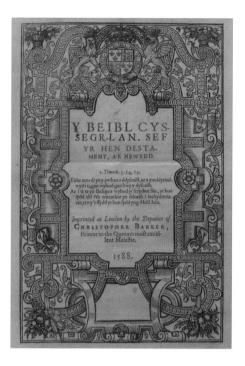

For centuries, the Church, in its various forms, has been a powerful force throughout Wales.

Its influence was felt in public life, politics and in shaping Welsh culture. The architecture of many great

churches, monasteries and cathedrals are an impressive part of the Welsh landscape; not least the romantic

Tintern Abbey, which has inspired so many artists and writers. The translation of the Bible into Welsh in 1588

not only allowed the people of Wales to worship in their native tongue, it was used to teach many

generations to read and write. In the process, the Welsh Bible became a cornerstone in the continuity of the

Welsh language. Later, in the 17th century, Nonconformist Protestantism flourished and in more recent times

the Methodist chapel became a familiar sight in the mining villages of South Wales.

The years of armed struggle with our neighbours not only left many major landmarks in Wales, but also helped to forge our sense of nationhood, which still prevails today. Offa's Dyke, constructed around 784 gave Wales for the first time a clear defined eastern boundary. Later, in 1301, the English King, Edward I made his son Prince of Wales, and aimed to unite Wales and England. To help secure his ambitions he embarked upon

an ambitious programme of castle building, including three great new edifices at Harlech, Conwy and

Caernarfon, which still largely survive. Full political union came some time later, under Henry VIII, with the

Acts of Union of 1536 and 1543. This Union has remained complete until the recent Act to create the

National Assembly, under which the people of Wales have regained some measure of self-government.

Conwy Castle, North Wales, a World Heritage site, and one of the fortresses commissioned by King Edward I

Folklore, legend and heritage are important to people in Wales. United with England since the sixteenth

century, we are proud of our history and individual identity. Owain Glyn Dŵr and the Princes of Wales remain

important figures in helping us to understand what it means to be Welsh. Today, Welsh heritage, from the

warrior Celts to the pinnacle of the coal industry, is celebrated. Many museums and galleries also seek to

explain what made Wales the nation it is today. The National Museum of Welsh Life shows many examples

of the way we lived, and visitor attractions such as the Big Pit Mining Museum and the Rhondda Heritage

Park aim to bring our history to life.

Case Study Owain Glyn Dŵr

As unrest grew into rebellion in the early years of the 15th century, Owain Glyn Dŵr emerged as the leader of the Welsh uprising against English rule. A descendent of the princes of Powys, Glyn Dŵr was crowned Prince of Wales at a parliament summoned to Machynlleth. By 1409 his rebellion was over, but Glyn Dŵr was not captured and his exact fate is unknown. His name has lived on in Welsh folklore.

(left) Statue of Owain Glyn Dŵr, by Alfred Turner, Cardiff, South Wales   *(above, top)* The Parliament House at Machynlleth, North Wales, the meeting place of the parliament summoned by Owain Glyn Dŵr

Much of our history is inextricably interwoven with our rich and intricate language. Like a golden thread it

weaves its way through the fabric of our past. We are proud that Welsh is probably the oldest living language in

Europe, and celebrate this in the National Eisteddfod. This is an eight-day cultural festival, which is held annually,

alternately in North and South Wales. It is the largest popular competitive festival of music and poetry in Europe, and

attracts over 170,000 visitors and 6,000 entrants every year. It is unique because it takes place entirely in Welsh.

Although a modern festival, its roots are based firmly in over 800 years of tradition. In many ways, it echoes the values

of modern Wales. Secure in our heritage, we are optimistic about the future, and aim to enjoy our new-found

confidence as a nation: prepared to take its rightful place in the world.

Chapter seven

CHERISHING OUR CULTURE

"In their rhymed songs and set speeches they so subtle and

ngenious that they produce, in their native tongue,

rnaments of wonderful and exquisite invention"

Giraldus Cambrensis, 1216

83

Gwlad, gwlad,

pleidiol wyf i'm gwlad!

Tra mor yn fur i'r bur hoff bau

O bydded i'r hen iaith barhau

Home, home, true am I to home, While seas secure the land so pure, Oh may the old language endure.
HEN WLAD FY NHADAU (THE LAND OF MY FATHERS) Chorus of the Welsh National Anthem

To a large extent, the distinct cultural heritage of Wales is a direct result of the Welsh language. From this

have flowed many of our great traditions such as the Eisteddfoddau: a spectacular celebration of the eternal

Welsh arts, oratory and musical skills. One of the enduring images of Wales is that of the Male Voice Choir.

Born in the coal mining valleys of South Wales in the mid-19th century, the choirs are internationally famous

for their close harmony singing. Many individual Welsh men and women have gained international

reputations. Composers like Ivor Novello, one of the finest songwriters in the British Isles; and singers such as

Bryn Terfel, Dame Gwyneth Jones, Dame Shirley Bassey, Tom Jones, all of whom continue to pack concert halls

the world over.

Case Study The Welsh language

A Celtic language, related to Breton and Cornish, Welsh is one of Europe's oldest surviving languages. Spoken by around 20% of the population, Welsh has equal status, by law, with English in Wales. The continued use of Welsh has helped Welsh culture to survive, particularly in its music and poetry.

(previous page) International singing sensation, Charlotte Church

The Welsh National Opera perform "Cavelleria Rusticana"

The BBC National Orchestra of Wales is the main focus for classical music and the performance of new work in Wales, the Welsh National Opera is regarded as one of the world's leading opera companies, and both of them perform extensively inside and outside Wales. Major arenas, including the Millennium Stadium in Cardiff, host a range of other events from pop concerts to jazz. Many of these feature the latest generation of highly talented Welsh performers, such as the Manic Street Preachers and the Stereophonics.

James Dean Bradfield, lead singer of the Manic Street Preachers

The national culture of Wales is refreshed by the vibrant media industry in Wales, which is spearheaded by

the Welsh-language TV station S4C, and BBC Wales. Wales continues to produce fine actors. Stars such as

Catherine Zeta-Jones, Ioan Gruffydd and Rhys Ifans follow a line of Welsh screen legends that include Richard

Burton and Sir Anthony Hopkins. In the world of literature Welsh talent includes Trezza Azzopardi whose

debut novel 'The Hiding Place' was nominated for the Booker Prize in 2000.

Case Study New Welsh Actors

From Ivor Novello, through Richard Burton, Desmond Llewellyn, and Stanley Baker, to stars like Ioan Gruffydd, Catherine Zeta-Jones and Rhys Ifans (pictured left), Welsh actors have always illuminated the stage and screen with outstanding performances.

(above) Cover of "The Hiding Place", the Booker-award nominated book by Cardiff-born author Trezza Azzopardi

Poetry, in both Welsh and English, is a great pillar of Welsh culture. Welsh

poets writing in English, such as R S Thomas and Dylan Thomas gained

worldwide reputations. Medieval poetry in Welsh is the source of many of the

myths and legends that abound throughout Wales.

Dylan Thomas, author of "Under Milk Wood"

Our love of sport extends far beyond rugby, and Welsh competitors excel in many fields.

From track and field to snooker, our athletes have won an enviable collection of gold medals and

championships. In 2002-2003, Welsh competitors and teams won 169 medals at World, European and

Commonwealth championships, including 31 medals at the Commonwealth games. In addition, Welsh

competitors and teams won 210 British Championships. Welsh Soccer stars such as Ryan Giggs and John

Hartson have performed at the highest level for their clubs. While we can't claim all the credit, there must

be something in our environment and heritage that encourages so many fine performances.

(left) Colin Jackson, twice winner of World Championship Gold medals in the 110m hurdles
(above, top) Tanni Grey-Thompson, winner of four Gold Medals at the Paralympics in Sydney, 2000
(above, middle) Mark Williams, world snooker No. 1   *(above, lower)* Kelly Morgan, UK women's badminton No.1

Rugby is perhaps the greatest Welsh passion. The nation was extremely proud to host the last great sporting event of the 20th century, the 1999 Rugby World Cup. Some group matches were held at three different venues in Wales, with the final in the Millennium Stadium, Cardiff.

This magnificent, world-class arena, costing over £100 million, includes a retractable roof, and, in addition to

rugby, stages all kinds of major sporting, music and arts events.

Argentina kick off against Wales in the first game of the 1999 Rugby World Cup, held in the Millennium Stadium, Cardiff, South Wales

Chapter eight

WALES. WORLD OF OPPORTUNITY

"Since coming into Wales he has found the country most marvellous and strange"

John de Weston to officers of the Prince of Wales, 1345

The Welsh Assembly Government has a strategic plan for Wales.

Two of its major themes are social inclusion: the development of an inclusive society where everyone has the

chance to fulfil their potential; and equal opportunities: the promotion of a culture in which diversity is

valued and equality of opportunity is a reality. There is a commitment to spread prosperity and well being

throughout Wales. Inequalities of all kinds will be reduced and the economy and society will become clearly

outward looking, well educated, healthy, skilled and creative. Such an economic and social environment will

create great opportunities for everyone living and working in Wales.

(previous page) Statue in the regenerated Cardiff Bay, South Wales
(left) Prince Charles, the Prince of Wales, at a graduation ceremony in Swansea, South Wales
(above, top) Students at Barry College, South Wales   (above, lower) Horticulture student, Mid Wales

While increasing economic prosperity is important, this cannot be at the expense of our environment.

We have inherited a beautiful land, but we must recognise that we are merely its guardians for future

generations. The wealth that we create must also promote enduring, balanced and beneficial change in our

communities and in our environment. Which is why achievement of sustainable development is the third key

theme of the strategic plan for Wales. New strategies are being developed for waste management and air quality;

for energy efficiency and for clean energy such as wind-generated electricity.

The improvements will not happen overnight, but there is an overwhelming commitment to achieving the

plan's objectives, and to bequeath an inheritance to future citizens that they will value and cherish; a quality

of life that will be the envy of the world.

Wind Turbines near Carno, Mid Wales

Case Study Centre for Alternative Technology, Machynlleth, North Wales

The Centre for Alternative Technology is concerned with the search for globally sustainable and ecologically sound technologies and ways of life. Its resident community is also committed to the implementation of the best achievable environmental practices. Visitors have the opportunity to learn, often through practical experience, about those technologies and ways of living which work with natural processes and are environmentally friendly.

Since devolution, the Welsh Assembly Government has set

out a vision of what the Wales of the 21st century will be:

• United, confident, outward-looking and creative

• Prosperous, well-educated, skilled, healthy, environmentally and culturally rich

• Served by modern, efficient and accessible public services

• Active in its local communities, where the voice of local people is heard

• Fairer – a place where everyone is valued

Already Wales and its people have achieved so much. We are drawing on the lessons of our heritage, informed by

the strengths of our culture to develop a uniquely Welsh approach to the challenges we face.

Challenges that we will meet so that Wales achieves its proper status of "World Nation".

ACKNOWLEDGMENTS AND CREDITS

The Welsh Assembly Government would like to thank everyone who helped in the preparation of this book.
Every effort has been made to trace the copyright holders of material used, and the details are given below.
The Welsh Assembly Government apologises for any unintentional omissions.

Foreword and Contents

 Courtesy of Deeside College

 Courtesy of the Wales Tourist Board Photolibrary

 © WDA

 Courtesy of the Wales Tourist Board Photolibrary

 Courtesy of the Wales Tourist Board Photolibrary

Chapter 1

 Page 3   © Paul Burnett

 Page 4   Courtesy of Airbus UK

 Page 5   Courtesy of IQE plc

 Page 5   © WDA

 Pages 6-7   Courtesy of the Wales Tourist Board Photolibrary

 Page 8   Courtesy of Mid Wales TEC Canolbarth Cymru

 Page 9   Courtesy of Barry College

 Page 9   Courtesy of CELTEC North Wales TEC

 Page 10   Courtesy of the Wales Tourist Board Photolibrary

 Pages 12-13 © Huw John

Chapter 2

 Page 15   © Huw Evans Picture Agency

 Pages 16-17 Crown Copyright

 Page 18,19 Courtesy of Western Mail and Echo

 Page 20   Photolibrary Wales © Jeff Morgan

Chapter 3

 Page 23   © Jeff Morgan/Wales Press Photo

 Page 24   Courtesy Ty Nant Water © Bethan Davies

 Page 25   © WDA

 Page 25   © WDA

 Pages 26-27 Courtesy of WDA

 Page 28   Courtesy of Big Pit Mining Museum

 Page 29   Courtesy of the Wales Tourist Board Photolibrary

 Page 29   © WDA

 Page 30   Courtesy of S4C

 Page 31   © SAF and Christmas Films

 Page 31   Courtesy of Cartwn Cymru

 Page 31   Courtesy of S4C

 Page 32   Courtesy of WDA

 Page 33   Courtesy of University of Wales, Swansea

 Page 34-35 Courtesy of WDA

Chapter 4

 Page 37   Photolibrary Wales © Dave Newbould

 Page 38   Courtesy of Celtic Manor Resort

 Page 39   Courtesy of the Wales Tourist Board Photolibrary

 Page 39   Courtesy of the Wales Tourist Board Photolibrary

 Pages 40-41 © Colin Molyneux

 Page 42   Courtesy of the Wales Tourist Board Photolibrary

 Page 43   © RSPB Images

 Page 43   Courtesy of the Wales Tourist Board Photolibrary

 Page 43   © Mick Baines

 Pages 44-45 Courtesy of the Wales Tourist Board Photolibrary

 Page 46   Courtesy of the Wales Tourist Board Photolibrary

 Page 47   Courtesy of the Wales Tourist Board Photolibrary

Page 47   Courtesy of the Wales Tourist Board Photolibrary

Page 47   Courtesy of the Wales Tourist Board Photolibrary

Pages 48-49 Courtesy of the Wales Tourist Board Photolibrary

Page 50   Courtesy of the Wales Tourist Board Photolibrary

Page 51   Courtesy of Cardiff Marketing

Page 51   Courtesy of the Wales Tourist Board Photolibrary

Pages 52-53 *Photolibrary Wales © David Williams*

Chapter 5

 Page 55 *Photolibrary Wales © Billie Stock*

 Page 56 *© WDA*

 Page 57 *Courtesy of Airbus UK*

 Page 58-59 *Courtesy of Thales Optics Coatings*

 Pages 60-61 *Cadw: Welsh Historic Monuments. Crown Copyright*

 Page 62 *© WDA*

 Page 63 *© WDA*

 Page 63 *© WDA*

 Page 63 *© WDA*

 Page 64 *Courtesy of Pinacl, Communication Systems*

 Page 65 *Courtesy of Euro DPC*

 Page 66 *Photolibrary Wales © David Williams*

 Page 67 *Courtesy of WDA*

 Page 67 *Courtesy of the Wales Tourist Board Photolibrary*

 Page 68-69 *Courtesy of the Wales Tourist Board Photolibrary*

Chapter 6

 Page 71 *© Harry Williams Photography*

 Page 72 *Courtesy of the Wales Tourist Board Photolibrary*

 Page 73 *Courtesy of the Wales Tourist Board Photolibrary*

 Page 73 *Courtesy of the Wales Tourist Board Photolibrary*

 Page 74 *Courtesy of the Wales Tourist Board Photolibrary*

 Page 75 *By permission of the National Library of Wales*

 Pages 76,77 *Cadw: Welsh Historic Monuments. Crown Copyright*

 Page 78,79 *Courtesy of Cardiff County Council*

 Page 79 *Courtesy of the Wales Tourist Board Photolibrary*

Page 80,81 *Photolibrary Wales © David Williams*

Chapter 7

 Page 83 *Courtesy of Sony Music Entertainment (UK) © Simon Fowler*

 Page 84,85 *© Phil Boorman*

 Pages 86-87 *Courtesy of Welsh National Opera*

 Pages 88-89 *Photolibrary Wales © Mike Thomas*

 Page 90,91 *Courtesy of Western Mail and Echo*

 Page 91 *Courtesy Macmillan Publishers Limited and Duke University © William Gedney*

 Pages 92-93 *© Hulton Archives*

 Page 94 *Allsports © Mike Powell*

 Page 95 *Allsports © Mike Hewitt*

 Page 95 *Allsports © Tom Shaw*

 Page 95 *Courtesy of Western Mail & Echo*

 Pages 96-97 *Allsports © Mike Hewitt*

Chapter 8

 Page 99 *© Travel Ink/Chris Stock*

 Page 100 *Courtesy of South Wales Evening Post*

 Page 101 *Courtesy of Barry College*

 Page 101 *Courtesy of Mid Wales TEC Canolbarth Cymru*

 Pages 102-103 *© Patricia Aithie/Ffotograff*

Pages 104-105 *Courtesy of the Wales Tourist Board Photolibrary*

Page 105 *Courtesy of the Wales Tourist Board Photolibrary*

Page 106 *Illustration by Mike Wall Crown Copyright*

Designed in Wales by Golley Slater & Partners

Printed in Wales by Cambrian Printers Ltd, Aberystwyth

ACKNOWLEDGMENTS AND CREDITS